—対訳—

世界平和の祈りの運動精神

— Bilingual Book —

The Principle Behind
The World Peace Prayer Movement

白光出版

418-0102

静岡県富士宮市 人穴 812-1

Published by Byakko Press

812-1 Hitoana, Fujinomiya-shi

Shizuoka-ken, Japan 418-0102

Homepage: http//:www.byakkopress.ne.jp

E-mail: editor@byakkopress.ne.jp

Printed in the USA and the UK by Booksurge.com

Homepage: http://www.booksurge.com

E-mail: info@booksurge.com

Translated from the Japanese

by Noriko Tatsuma and Mary McQuaid

Edited by David W. Edelstein

英訳：立間 紀子／監訳：マクエイド・メアリ

Designed by Hiromi Ohta

ISBN 4-89214-158-5

— 対訳 —
世界平和の祈りの運動精神

— *Bilingual Book* —
The Principle Behind
The World Peace Prayer Movement

五井 昌久

Masahisa Goi

Byakko Press

五井昌久の著書

神と人間

老子講義

人類の未来

その他多数

by the same author

God and Man

The Spirit of Lao Tsu

The Future of Mankind

and others

世界平和の祈りの運動精神

個人と人類とのつながり

　この人間世界は、病気と貧乏と争いとがなかったらどんなに良いであろう、とは誰でも思うことでありましょう。まして、自分や自分の周囲の者が、病気をし貧乏をし、争いごとでみちていた、という経験をもっている人は、殊更に強くこうした悪いことの無い世界を願うに違いありません。

　過去からの聖者賢者たちは、老病貧苦をこの世からもあの世からも、すっかり消し去ってしまいたい、という深い願いをもって、世の指導者となったのであります。
　愛深い人々は、そうした人類の苦悩を和らげる為に役立つことを願って、或る人は医者に、或る人は広い意味の科学者に、或るいは社会運動家として、その身を挺身してゆくのであります。

　病気や貧乏は個人的なものであり、争いごとの大きなもの、つまり戦争は、国家的人類的なものだ、と思っている人もあると思いますが、病気や貧乏も、只単なる個

The Principle behind
The World Peace Prayer Movement

Relationship between the Individual and Humanity

"If there were no disease, no poverty, and no struggle, what a pleasant place this world would be." I think that almost everyone feels this way. In particular, people who have come in close contact with disease, poverty, or incessant struggles, either in their own lives or in the lives of others, surely wish even more strongly for a world free from those negative conditions.

And so, for many ages, saints and wise people have become guides for human society because they deeply wished to free this world, and the world after death, from all illness, poverty, anguish, and infirmities of aging. Others, motivated by a deep spirit of love, have tried to help diminish human suffering by working in fields such as science and medicine, or by devoting themselves to various social endeavors.

On the other hand, there are also people who feel that disease and poverty are personal matters, and that only large disputes like wars should concern the nation or hu-

人的なものではなくて、社会国家人類という、大きな集団の影響下にその原因が起り得る、ということがあるのですし、それを直し得る力も、大きな集団の力によって為し得るものなのです。

　今日の生活は、個人と国家や人類とが密接不離なる関係をもっておりまして、個人はもはや、単なる個人ではなく、大きな集団の一つの単位としての個人なのであります。

　ですから愛深い人々は、常に個々人を通し、集団集団を通して、全人類の為の奉仕にその一生を捧げつくしているわけなのです。それが宗教の面においてであろうと、科学の面であろうと、政治の面においてであろうと、その根底は等しく人類愛の心によって為されているのであります。

　実際に今日のように、地球が狭く感じられることは過去の時代にはなかったことです。米国の出来事が同時に、日本においても見聞きできるというテレビの発達、航空機による旅行時間の短縮等々、他国のことが我がことのように感じられる程、距離や時間が短くなってきているのです。私共の感覚の上で確かに地球は狭くなったのであり、他国と自国との距たりが縮められていっているのです。

manity as a whole. I contend, however, that disease and poverty are not just personal matters. The causes of such conditions can stem from the influence of a large mass of people, be it a society, a nation, or the entire world population. And for precisely that reason the power to remedy them also resides with a large mass of people.

Our present life entails closely-knit relationships between the individual, the nation, and humanity. In this sense, an individual is not just a mere individual any more, but is one participant in a large group.

That is why people with a deeply loving nature continue to dedicate their lives to humanity by working at the individual level and through various groups. Whether their services are offered through religion, science, or politics, all of them share the same spirit of humanitarian love.

In past eras, the people of the world never felt so closely linked together as we do today. With the development of television, we can see and hear about events in other countries right away, without leaving our own homes. Airplanes have shortened our travel time immensely. In ways like these, the gaps in time and space between people have become so small that we feel as though the conditions in other countries are our very own. In terms

　それは善いことの上にも、悪いことの上にも、実現されているのであります。文明文化の速やかなる交流、これは喜ぶべきことでありますが、他国において行われたる核爆弾の実験による放射能は、直ちに我が国にもその影響を及ぼしてくるのであり、他国の伝染病なども、すぐに我が国をおびやかすことになるのです。まして、密接なる関係をもつ米国内の出来事は我が国の経済状態に微妙な影響を与えるのであります。

心の世界もみなつながっている

　それは、あたかも太平洋の水が、日本と米国とを一つに結んでいると同じように、空においても、想念波動の世界においても、世界は全く一つにつながっているのです。

　海の水がつながっていることや、空が一つであることなどは、すぐに理解できるが、想念波動がつながっているということはどういうことか、という問がでてくると思います。

　ところがこの想念波動の問題を知ることこそ、世界平和を実現する最も大事なことなのであります。想念波動

of our senses, the world has certainly become smaller, and the distance between other countries and our own has been getting shorter and shorter.

This drawing together of the world has both good and bad sides. The speedy exchange of culture and civilization is something worth encouraging. But the radioactivity resulting from nuclear weapon tests in other countries can instantly produce effects in our own country. Contagious or infectious diseases in other countries can immediately be perceived as menaces to our own. Even the domestic events in other countries have a subtle influence on our own country's economic and political conditions.

Our Thoughts are also Linked

Just as the water of the oceans links the continents, the world's people are completely linked via the air and also in the world of thought vibrations.

People can readily understand that the water of the ocean is joined together, or that the sky is one entity, but a question may arise as to the meaning of "thought vibrations being linked to each other."

Why do we need to know about thought vibrations? I suggest that knowing about thought vibrations is highly

の伝わりということは、音波や電波や光波によってテレ
ビやラジオやテレフォンで、お互いの声を聞き、他国の
人の姿をみることができるという科学の原理と同じなの
です。想念波動とは電波や光波や音波よりも、もっと微
妙な精神宇宙子の波動なのであります。

　これは私たちが現在研究中の宇宙子科学[1]の原理に
よってよく判ることなのですが、まだ一般の知識として
は、この精神宇宙子のことは判っておりませんので、電
波や音波光波よりもっと微妙な波動とだけ思って頂けれ
ばよいでしょう。

　この微妙な波動が、人類すべての思い思いの波動と
なって、世界中を空気の波のように無限の層となって蔽
いつくしているのです。その波動は、争いに充ちたもの
もあり、妬みに充ちたものもあり、病苦、貧苦に充ちた
ものもあり、恨みや怒りに充ちたものもあります。また
そうした暗い汚れた想念波動でない、明るい愛に充ちた、
善意に充ちた光明そのものの波動もあるのであります。

　こうした想念波動の渦は、それぞれがエネルギーであ

important for the development of world peace.

Many people have a sense of how sound, radio and light waves function through the media of television, radio, and telephones, enabling us to hear each other's voices and see images of people in other places. Thought vibrations travel according to the same scientific principle that underlies these processes. A thought vibration is a wave of spiritual, cosmic waves more subtle than radio, light, or sound waves.

This has been made quite clear to us through the principles of cosmic science,[1] which we have been researching for some years now. But as cosmic vibrations have not yet become general knowledge, I would like you to simply think of a cosmic vibration as a wave finer than radio, sound, or light waves.

The various kinds of thought waves generated by humanity cover the earth, forming infinite layers, like waves of air. Among those vibrations, some are filled with strife, some with envy, some with the anguish of illness or poverty, and some with resentment or anger. At the same time, others are not dark or impure, but filled with brightly shining love and good intentions. Those are the vibrations of bright light itself.

When electric energy flows, it turns into a current of

りまして、そのエネルギーは人間の肉体に働きかけて、人間にその想念波動の通りの行為をなさしめるのです。電気的エネルギーが流れ出せば、電流となってモーターを動かし得ると同じように、想念波動のエネルギーも、人間の肉体を動かし得るのです。

そして、その想念波動が争いや妬みの暗い汚れたものであれば、働きかけられた人間はそういう行為をするのであり、愛や善意の光明波動であれば、愛の行為になってくるのであります。

人間の肉体というものは、肉眼で見、肉の手で触れれば固まった一定した形をもったもので、口から入らなければ外部のものが中に入ってくることはないようにみえますが、実は常に外部から眼に見えぬ種々な要素が入ってきているのです。

眼から耳からは、映像として文字として言葉として音として入り、放射能のようなものは体のいたるところから体内に沁み通ってきます。そのように、光線よりもっと微妙である想念の波動は、直接に脳髄に入りこんでくるのであり、神経系統のあらゆるところにも沁みこんでくるのです。

ですから、人類世界のすべての階層のそれぞれの想念波動は、各個人や集団のそれと合致した想念の渦をもつ

electricity, making it possible to start a motor. In the same way, the energy of thought waves can activate a person's physical body. Each swirl of thought vibrations has its own kind of energy. This energy works on the physical body, and causes the person to act in a way that corresponds with those thought waves.

If a thought vibration is dark and impure, filled with strife and envy, the person being controlled by it will act in a corresponding way. If it is a bright light vibration of love and good will, it will result in an action of love.

When we see it with our physical eyes or touch it with our physical hands, a human being's physical body seems to be solid, with a certain shape. It appears that nothing enters the body from the outside except through the mouth, the pores, and so on. But in fact, various invisible elements are constantly entering from the outside.

Through our eyes and ears, we receive images, letters, words, and sounds. But things like radioactivity permeate the body everywhere. Thought vibrations, which are finer than light waves, directly permeate the brain and every part of the nervous system.

All the various thought vibrations emitted by the whole of humanity, from all social strata and all walks

ところに、絶え間なく入りこんできて、その人やその集団は、恨みなら恨み、怒りなら怒り、争いなら争い、情欲なら情欲の渦中からぬけ出せないようになってしまうのであります。

人類愛欠如の原因

たまたまは愛の心や柔和な想いが起ってきても、争いや恨みの暗い想念波動の渦巻が烈しすぎると、そうした善なる想念もたちまち流し去られて、その個人や集団はまた再び暗黒想念を出しつづけてしまうのであります。

それはちょうど、暴力団に入ってしまった少年が、これはいけないと気づいて、その仲間からぬけ出ようとしても、その団員たちの脅迫にあって、どうしてもぬけ出せない、というのと同じようなものです。

of life, are constantly merging with corresponding kinds of thought vibrations. Just imagine one person, or one group of people, having its own swirl of thought vibrations, and similar kinds of thought vibrations from all sectors of humanity being drawn to that swirl and merging with it. If that person or group has thoughts of resentment, or anger, or struggle, or lust, the spinning motion of those thought vibrations is intensified when it is joined by the same kinds of vibrations from all across humanity. This makes it almost impossible for the person or group to free itself from that spinning whirlpool.

How did we Lose the Spirit of Love?

Although a person may once in a while feel the spirit of love, or have kindhearted thoughts, those good thoughts can be swept away if the whirlpools of dark thought vibrations (struggle and grudges) surrounding the person are too violent. Then, that individual (or that group) will once again begin to emit dark thoughts.

This is similar to the situation of a boy who has joined a violent gang or terrorist organization. Even if he realizes that what they are doing is wrong, and tries to leave the group, he finds himself unable to leave when faced with threats from the other members. Once a vicious

　世界各国の軍備態勢というものと同様なものでありまして、武力による力と力の均こうによってのみ平和が保たれる、という考えは、お互いの優位を保つ為に、お互いの武力を増強させつづけなければならぬ、という悪循環をもたらし、何にもまして軍備に資金をついやすという状態になってしまい、それでいて、一日として安心していられる日のない、戦争恐怖症の人々をつくりあげている始末なのであります。

　これは世界にとって最も不幸なる、人間不信感の暗黒想念に踊らされている状態でありまして、世界の指導者がみなこんな心の状態では、とても世界の平和など及びもつかないことなのであります。

　軍備を増強して相手方を抑圧しようなどという考えのどこに、人類愛の想念がありましょうか、人間は生命において一つのものである、という人間本来の愛の心は、こうした差別心や不平等の想念からは、とても実行でき得るものではありません。

　こうした人類愛の欠如は、この人類世界を蔽っている

circle is set in motion, it is not so easy to put a stop to it or extract oneself from it.

Consider, for example, the military situation of each country. The idea has been set in motion that peace can be maintained only through a balance of military power. In order to attain military superiority, each side thinks it has to keep expanding its military power, and make military spending its number one priority. This kind of vicious circle produces people who constantly fear the outbreak of war, and cannot live even one day in peace.

This is the most miserable situation for the world to be in. It is a situation where people are manipulated by dark, distrustful thoughts. If all of the world leaders are in this mental state, world peace will be totally out of reach.

Where can we find the spirit of humanitarian love within the notion of suppressing others with increased military force? When they hold on to this kind of idea, which discriminates between the "self" and "others," people can never put the original human spirit of love into practice. I say this because "the original human spirit of love" essentially means that all human beings are originally one within the all-encompassing life of the universe.

The reason for this lack of humanitarian love is that

想念波動が、争いや恨みや憎悪に充ちているからなのであります。人間は本来神の分生命で、悪や不幸の想念をもっていない存在者なのですが、神の分生命であることを忘れてしまった人々が、神の光明波動に自ら遠ざかってしまって、その光明波動の薄れたところから、真理を見失いはじめて、現在のような善と悪との混淆した世界をつくりあげてしまったのです。

　この光明波動の薄れが、次第に暗黒化してきて、人間不信感の争いや妬みや憎悪の感情想念が生れ出で、地球最大の危機を迎えてしまったのであります。

想念波動の重大性

　こうした危機を救うには一体どうしたらよいのでしょう。どんな方法を用いたらよいのでしょう。武力の増強をつづけてあくまで、力の均衡でやってゆけばよいのでしょうか、それではいつまでたっても、人類から戦争の恐怖は去ることはありません。去るどころではなく、いつかは実際に世界大戦がはじまってしまうでしょう。

the thought vibrations of humanity are filled with strife, grudges, and hatred. Although human beings are originally lives that branch out from one divine source, and are free from any thought of evil or unhappiness, almost everyone on Earth has forgotten this. When they forgot it, they distanced themselves from the bright light vibration of their divine source. And because their consciousness had drifted to a place where bright light vibrations were sparse, they began to lose sight of the truth, and built a world mingling good with evil, like the world we see today.

As the bright light vibrations became sparse, people's thoughts gradually turned dark and gloomy. This led to distrustful feelings, strife, jealousy and hatred. And now, as a result, we have come to face the Earth's greatest crisis.

The Importance of Thought Vibrations

What can be done to overcome this crisis? What methods should we choose? Would it be best for each country to endlessly continue building its military to maintain a balance of power? If we do that, humanity will never be free from the terror of war. Even worse, a world war might really break out someday.

　人間の心には、造ったものは使ってみたい、強めた力は試してみたい、という想いがあるのでして、いつか何かのはずみで、核兵器のボタンを押さないとは限らないのであります。

　私はこゝで、今まで申し上げてきた、想念波動の重大性ということについて、皆さんにじっくり考えていただきたいと思うのです。想念波動を浄化しきらない限り、世界は絶対に平和になることはない、ということです。そして世界が平和にならない以上は、個人の平安はあり得ないということです。

　たとえ、病気が直ったとしても、貧乏から一時ぬけでたとしても、それだけで、その個人が平安になったというわけにはゆきません。それは一時の平安でありまして、永遠の平安ではありません。

　私は個人の平安と、世界人類との完全平和が、一つにつながってなされる、という方法を願い求めたのです。そして生れ出たのが世界平和の祈りなのであります。

　個人個人の体は、肉体としてはお互いが離れてあるように見えますが、想念波動の世界ではお互いが結び合い交流し合って、お互いに影響を及ぼしあっているのです。それは、親子兄弟とか、親戚知人とかいう間柄だけでは

Human beings tend to feel that once they have built something they want to use it, or that once they have strengthened their power they want to try it out. And at some point, by some chance, someone might press the button and activate nuclear weapons.

Here I would like to ask all of you to carefully think over the importance of thought vibrations, which are the key issue here. Unless our thought vibrations are completely purified, there can be absolutely no way for this world to attain peace. And unless peace prevails on earth, there can be no peace for the individual either. I say this because, even if one's illness has been cured, or one has temporarily escaped from poverty, that alone does not mean that one has found peace. It is a short-term peace, not a peace that lasts forever.

I have sought and asked for a method through which individual serenity and complete peace on earth can be linked together and achieved at the same time. What emerged as a result were the prayer words "May Peace Prevail on Earth."

Although physically, each person appears to be separate from others, in the world of thought vibrations we are all connected, interrelating with and influencing one another. These links exist not only among parents, chil-

なく、一個人の想念波動は一瞬一瞬の間にも地球上を経巡っているのであります。

　ラジオやテレビに伝わってくる音波や光波は、絶え間なく大気中を流れているのでありますが、ラジオやテレビのスイッチをひねって電流を流し入れ、ダイヤルをそれぞれの音波や光波に合わせなければ、そこになんの音も聞えず、なんの映像も写ってこないのです。

　人間の想念波動も全くそれと同じでありまして、自己の出した波動が地球上を経巡っていると同時に、すべての人類の想念波動は、自分の上に流れてきているのであります。ただ自己は、自己の意識、意識といっても表面に出ている顕在意識だけではなく、潜在している潜在意識を含めた想念波動の部分のダイヤルをひねっていることになるのです。

個人と人類が同時に救われなければ

　そこで、人類すべての想念波動が自分の上に蔽いかぶさってきているのですけれど、自己の廻しているダイヤルの分だけ、自己の運命となって現われてくるのであり

dren, brothers, sisters, relatives and friends — they exist among all the people who share similar thought vibrations. An individual's thought vibrations circulate round the earth in the space of an instant, reaching everyone who has an affinity for them.

Let me explain this point a bit further. Sound and light waves, transmitted via radio or television, are constantly flowing through the air. But unless you switch on the equipment to start the electric current, and adjust the dials to receive the various sound or light waves, no sound will be heard and no images will be projected there.

Human thought vibrations are exactly the same. While the vibrations we have emitted are travelling round the earth, the thought vibrations of all humanity are flowing toward us at the same time. We tune in to them with our consciousness. When I say "consciousness" here, I do not mean only the surface consciousness, which we normally call "consciousness." I am also talking about the hidden consciousness called the "subconscious."

Simultaneously Uplifting the Individual and Humanity

The thought vibrations of all humanity are circulating all around us, but only those we are "dialing" or "tuning in to" will influence the course of our lives. In other

ます。これをいいかえますと、自己の出している想念が憎悪や争いの想念波動であれば、その想念波動は、同じような想念波動をもっている地球上の多くの人々の上に影響を及ぼしているのであります。そして、この想念波動が、愛や善意の光明波動であれば、地球人の多くの人々は、その光明波動によって、知らぬ間に浄められているわけなのです。

　この真理を考えますと、個人の想念行為は、自己にその報いが必ずやってくると同時に、人類全般にその影響を及ぼしていることになるので、どんな小さな想念行為でもゆるがせにできないのであります。

　私はこの真理をよく知っておりますので、個人と人類が同時に救われなければ、世界は平和になることはないと言っているのです。個人個人の想念の在り方を問題にしないでいて、世界平和も戦争は嫌だもあるものではありません。戦争が嫌な人は、先ず自己の想念を、平和な調和したものにしておくことを心がけなければいけません。

　戦争反対を叫び、世界平和を叫びながら、その運動を闘争という名で呼んだりしている団体や、自己の団体の

words, if the thoughts you emit are waves of hatred and struggle, those vibrations will influence many people in the world who have thoughts of hatred and struggle. On the other hand, if your thoughts are bright light waves of love and good will, they will influence many people who have thought vibrations of love and good will. On top of that, because all human beings essentially consist of light, everyone in this world will be unconsciously purified by the flow of your brightly shining thoughts.

When you think about this principle, you can see that even the smallest thought activity cannot be neglected. Its effects will surely come back to the individual, while at the same time influencing humanity in general.

Because I am thoroughly aware of this truth, I can clearly state that we will never have peace on Earth until both humanity and the individual are simultaneously up-lifted and set free from dark thought vibrations. Unless we address the subject of each individual's thinking, and of what kind of thinking would be most beneficial, it is out of the question to talk about world peace or how we dislike war. If we dislike war, then before anything else we have to turn our own thoughts to peace and harmony.

There are some political and social groups which shout out their opposition to war and clamor for world

権力を強めることのみに全力を挙げていて、大自然の法則そのものである、調和の精神を踏みにじっている宗教団体などがあることそのものが、暗黒業想念の所産なのであります。

　個人の平安と世界人類の平和を達成する為には、憎悪や妬みや権力欲等々の業想念波、暗黒想念波動を、大光明波動によって浄めさらなければならないのです。

心の光明化は環境の光明化

　個人が自己の運命を改善するのには、自己の運命の上に現われている、自分の欲っしない状態、例えば病気や貧乏や恨みや妬みや恐怖の想いなどの不調和な状態を、自分の心から放す練習をしなければなりません。そうした自己の欲っしない状態を自己の上から放つ為にはどうしたらよいのでしょう。

peace, calling their movement a "struggle" or a "fight." There have also been some misdirected religious groups which devote all their energy to reinforcing their authority, while at the same time trampling on the harmonious spirit which is the law of great nature itself. Far from being "peace movements," these kinds of activities are nothing more than manifestations of dark thought vibrations.

To attain peace for both humanity and the individual, dark thought vibrations such as hatred, jealousy, and a thirst for power have to be purified by waves of bright light.

Brightening our Minds and our Environment

To make a better future for oneself as an individual, one must practice letting go of unwelcome thoughts and attitudes. In saying "unwelcome thoughts and attitudes," I am referring to thoughts and attitudes which are disagreeable and unharmonious, such as thinking about being ill, thinking about being poor, or harboring feelings like resentment, envy and fear. Thoughts and attitudes like these disrupt your mental and physical harmony, and also the harmony of Earth. What can you do to free your mind from these unwanted thoughts and attitudes?

　それは、潜在意識と顕在意識とにかかわらず、自己の運命環境に現われた状態は、自己の想念波動の上に必ずあるのでありますから、これは自分の想いの中にこういう運命環境になるべき原因があるのだ、と思いを明らかにして、自己の想念を明るい幸せな方向にむけてしまうことが大事なのです。どうすればよいかといいますと、今、自己に現われている現象は、すべて過去世から現在に至る誤った想念の消えてゆく姿だ、と思って、改めて新しく、自己の欲っする状態や想念を出してゆけばよいのです。

　しかし、いちいち自己の欲っする状態を考え出している余裕はありません。

　そこで、積極的に、世界人類の平和を願うという、自己にとっても人類全部にとっても、一番根本の問題である、世界平和の祈りの中に自己の天命の完うされることの願いと共に、自己の全想念を投入してしまうことに想いを定めるのです。そして自分の心に現在の環境に対する不平や、自己の性癖に対する不満が起る度びに、その不平不満を、世界平和の祈りの中に、消えてゆく姿として入れてしまうようにするのです。

The key is to turn your thoughts in a bright and positive direction. How can you do this? The method which I propose is to think of all the bad conditions and events taking place within us and around us as the vanishing reverberations of mistaken thoughts from a past consciousness. After that, the next step is to think of the bright situation that you wish for, and to keep on creating more and more bright new thoughts.

However, we do not have enough time to think of every little detail of each situation that we wish for.

In view of this, I suggest that you make up your mind to aggressively throw all your thoughts into the prayer "May Peace Prevail on Earth," since world peace is the most fundamental issue for you and for humanity as a whole. At the same time, I would also suggest that you keep wishing for your own divine missions to be accomplished. Then, each time they come to mind, try to fling all of your complaints about your present situation, as well as your dissatisfaction with your own personality and habits, straight into the prayer for world peace.

Just keep reminding yourself that those old thoughts and feelings are being transformed through the bright

　そう致しますと、いつの間にか知らぬ間に、自己の想念波動が、明るい調和したものに変化していって、平安な感情になってまいります。すると、それにつれて生活環境も明るく幸せなものに次第に変わってくるのであります。

　これは当然なことであります。何故かと申しますと、自己の出していた想念波動で知らぬ間に自己の運命をつくりあげていたのですから、その想念波動が、世界人類の平和を祈るというような、明るい大きな広いひびきに変わった以上、世界平和の祈りに叶った明るい大らかな平安な環境が生れてくるのは、大自然の法則の通りなのであります。

　まして、世界平和の祈りというのは、大救世主を中心とした救世の神々の大光明波動から生れてきた祈りなので、この祈り言に想いの波長を合わせれば、救世の大光明波動は、その人の霊体に幽体に肉体にひびきわたって、その人の環境を光明化し、その人の周囲を光明波動で照してくれるのであります。

vibrations of the prayer words "May Peace Prevail on Earth."

As you continue to do this, before you know it your thought vibrations will become bright and harmonious, and you will begin to have a peaceful feeling. Consequently, your daily life will gradually become brighter and happier.

This only stands to reason, since, unconsciously, you had created your own circumstances with the thought vibrations which you had emitted. So, once you change them into the bright, expansive vibrations of world peace prayers, it is only natural for a proportionately bright, expansive, and peaceful situation to come about. This spontaneously happens through the laws of nature.

Why is it that more and more people are awakening to the need to pray for world peace? It is because, deep within their minds, their spiritual selves know that the time has come for this world to either achieve harmony or face destruction. Their inner selves know that their world peace prayers connect them with the tremendous power of countless celestial beings who are tirelessly working to guide this planet away from destruction. If you attune your thoughts to this prayer, the immense light of this large divine assembly will radiate through

　この世もあの世も、すべて神のみ心と想念波動とでできているので、その想念波動が、神のみ心のひびきに合致すれば、その人の心は光明化するにきまっているのです。そしてその人の心が光明化すれば、その人の環境も光明化してくることは理の当然なのであります。

　こうして個人が光明化することは、それがそのまま人類全般の上にも影響を及ぼすことになるので、それだけ地球上の暗黒想念が浄まることになるのです。

想念の浄化運動が主体

　私たちのやっている世界平和の祈りの運動は、想念波動の浄化ということが主であるわけで、世界人類の想念波動が浄まらなければ、世界平和は決してできるものではない、と思っているわけです。

　物質欲や権力欲で対立している場合は、それそのものが誤りであることはすぐ判りますが、思想と思想との対立というものは、どちらの思想にも、それぞれの理があ

all planes of your being, whether spiritual, subconscious, or physical. And it will, of course, also brighten your surroundings with its light waves.

This present world, as well as the world after death, is composed of two elements. One is thought waves, and the other is light vibrations from our divine source. If a person's thought waves match with those original, divine light vibrations, the person's attitude is bound to become brighter. And if one's attitude is brightened, it naturally follows that one's surroundings will also be brightened.

If even one individual is brightened, it will instantly produce an influence upon all of humanity, and the dark thought waves of this world will be purified to that very same extent.

Purifying Thought Waves is the Main Principle

The main principle behind the world peace prayer movement is to purify thought waves. A growing number of people are now putting this principle into practice. I feel sure that unless humanity's thought waves are purified, we will never be able to attain world peace.

We can easily see that it is wrong to oppose others out of greed for material things or a thirst for power. But when people oppose each other over differing ideas,

りまして、それぞれの思想に同感するものが、お互いに相対した集団となってくるので、どちらにも理がありながら、結果的には、世界を二分し三分してしまう不調和想念波動を世界中に流してしまうのであります。

　これは宗教団体の場合にも全く同じことがいえるので、自己集団の教えを固執していますと、教えそのものは別に悪くないとしても、神のみ心の一番根本のものである大調和精神に反して、他宗団との不調和をきたすのです。

　世界平和の祈りの運動精神は、すべての想念事柄を、ひとまず、神のみ心そのものである、大調和の中に入れきってしまおうとする運動なのであります。各自各国、種々様々な思想ややり方があるではありましょうが、一番大事なことは、この地球世界を滅亡させないことにあるのですから、枝葉末節的な方法や手段は後廻しにして、世界平和という人類の大願目の中に、一人でも一国でも多くの人々の想念を結集してゆかねばならぬと思っているのです。

each of their ideas seems to have a reasonable basis, so it does not strike people as wrong to form groups with people who share their ideas, and to stand in opposition to groups having other ideas. Consequently, in spite of the reasonable philosophies held by all sides, people end up emitting divisive thought waves which split the world into several parts.

The same can be said about religious groups. If you become rigidly attached to the doctrines of your own religious group, it can lead to disharmonious relationships with other religions. Even though the religious doctrines themselves are not wrong or bad, this discordant attitude goes against the fundamental divine spirit of infinite love and all-encompassing harmony.

The principle behind the world peace prayer movement is for people to set aside their differences for the time being and fully immerse all their thoughts and circumstances in the vibrations of perfect harmony which are, in other words, the existence of God itself. Although each individual or country may have worthwhile ideas and methods of their own, I feel that it is important to focus the thoughts of as many individuals and as many countries as possible on world peace, since world peace is the one, large-scale goal of humanity. Our first priority is

　枝葉末節的な小さな自我欲望を出していると、自己も人類も、暗黒想念波動に巻きこまれていって、遂いには破滅してしまわねばならなくなります。自分の方が正しいのだ、自国の方が正義なのだ、という正義のやりとりも、そのやりとりによって、お互いの心に怒りや憎しみの想念が湧きあがるようなものであったら、その正義感は、もう神のみ心そのものではなくなっているのです。

　ここのところを世の指導者たちは心をいたさなければいけないと思います。地球を滅亡させてしまって、なんの正義でありましょう。自国の利益も人類の利益も共に消滅してしまうのであります。

　人類の生命を尊重するのは、直接相手を傷つけ痛めなければよいというだけではなく、相手の生命を生き生きとさせてやる、ということにあるのです。お互いの生命が、神のみ心のままに生き生きと働けるような、お互いの天命が完うされるような、そういう個人であり、そういう国家であるように、私たちは、自他共にならなければいけないのです。

　それには何度も繰りかえすようですが、世界平和の祈

to prevent the Earth from falling apart completely. If we are to accomplish this, secondary details will have to be set aside for a later time.

When people continuously send out the petty desires of their own egos, both they as individuals and the nation as a whole become enveloped in swirls of dark thought waves, which can only lead to collapse. Likewise, if feelings of anger and hatred crop up during an exchange of views on justice, with each party insisting that it is in the right, or that one country has justice on its side, their sense of justice has already departed from the harmony of the universal law.

World leaders need to give careful consideration to this point. What is the good of debating over justice if this world perishes? The interests of one's own country, as well as the interests of humanity, will cease to exist.

To respect human life does not simply mean to avoid hurting people's feelings directly. It means to refresh and enliven other people's lives. Now is the time for all people and nations to work together actively, following the directives of their inner, divine mind. In this way, each individual and each nation will be able to accomplish its own role in creating world peace.

To this end, I would like to stress again the importance

りが大事なのであります。

世界人類が平和でありますように、私達の天命が完うされますように、という祈り心が大事なのであります。

　世界中の想念を、ひとまず、完全平和を願う祈り心に結集してしまうことが、何事にもまして大事なのです。各国各人の損得はその後で話し合えばよいことなのです。世界中の人たちの誰一人として望んでいない地球の滅亡に追いやるような、第三次大戦の勃発を防ぐことこそ、何国何民族であろうとも、人間一人一人の大きな責任である筈です。

人類の一人としての責任を自覚しよう

　その大きな責任を果たすためには、自分たちの欲望はひとまず後廻しにしてもよいではありませんか、地球が滅びてしまって、一体どこで自己の欲望を果たそうというのでしょう。自分一人ぐらい何をしたとて、世界人類となんのかかわりもないなどと思っていることは、とんでもない間違いです。

of prayer for world peace.

May peace prevail on Earth.
May peace be in our homes and countries.
May our missions be accomplished.

Before doing anything else, we need to pause for a while and focus the whole world's attention on a prayer that draws out the spirit of perfect peace on earth. After that, countries and individuals can talk of profit or loss.

Every person, whatever country or whatever ethnic group they may belong to, ought to feel a great sense of responsibility for preventing the outbreak of World War III. No one in the world wishes for that, as it would inevitably bring the Earth's existence to an end.

Our Responsibility as Members of Humanity

To fulfill this great responsibility, let us make up our minds to set aside our own self-oriented desires and ambitions for a later time. After all, where can we go to satisfy our ambitions if the Earth perishes? And if you think that, as one person, whatever you might do will have no influence on humanity, you are making a serious mistake.

　人間一人一人の想念行為が、今日程大事な時は他の時代にはなかったのです。前から申しておりますように、一人の人間の想念が暗黒想念（自分勝手な欲望）であるか、光明波動（愛と真の心）であるかによって、世界人類の運命は、滅亡にも完全平和にもなり得るのであります。

　昔からいわれる宗教の極意である、善にも悪にも把われず、今日このままをすべて素直に受けてゆこう、今日このままの姿は、つけ足すところも、減ずるところもない、神のみ心そのままの世界なのだ、という教えを更に一歩進んで、実在世界の完全円満な相を、世界平和の祈り言を通して、一日も早く、しかも、最少の苦悩の経験によって、この世に顕現せしめよう、という、大救世主のみ心を、私はこの肉体を通して、多くの人々に宣布実践しているのであります。

　今日、世界平和の祈りが日本において生れ出でたことこそ、神のみ心そのものなのでありまして、この祈り心によって、世界人類の暗黒的業想念波動が、次第に光明波動に浄められてゆくのであります。どうぞ皆さんもこ

There has never been a time when each person's thought activity has been as important as it is today. Depending on just one person's thoughts, humanity could veer toward either complete peace or destruction. You can choose whether your thoughts will emit bright waves of love and sincerity, or dark waves of egoistic desires.

Since ancient times, it has been said that the point of spiritual faith is not to be caught up in good or in evil, but to see that the world's present situation came about because the divine will allowed it to, as one step in a process toward carrying out the universal divine plan — that there is nothing to add and nothing to take away — and to accept everything as it is. I am taking this teaching one step further. Through prayer for world peace, let the divine blueprint for a peaceful world be perfectly manifested as soon as possible, with the smallest possible amount of suffering. This is the desire of the inner soul of each human being. Through my own existence, I am putting this teaching into practice and am striving to let more and more people know about it.

As part of the harmonious movement of the great universe, this prayer, "May Peace Prevail on Earth," has emerged at this precise time and place. Through the activity of this prayer, the dark vibrations surrounding

の真理をよく噛みしめられて、より一層世界平和の祈り
の運動に邁進して頂きたいのであります。

「神は沈黙していない」（白光出版　１９６７年）より

脚注
1．宇宙子科学の研究は五井昌久の提唱により始められ、
現在は世界平和運動の継承者である西園寺昌美に引き継
がれている。

世界平和の祈り

世界人類が平和でありますように
日本が平和でありますように
私達の天命が完うされますように
守護霊様ありがとうございます
守護神様ありがとうございます

humanity will gradually be purified and transformed into waves of bright light. I would like to ask each one of you to contemplate this truth well, and to let your life flow forward in tune with the movement of the world peace prayer.

from *God Is Not Sleeping*, Byakko Press, 1967
(English publication pending)

Note
1. The study of cosmic science was initiated by Masahisa Goi and is now conducted under the direction of his successor, Masami Saionji.

著者紹介

五井 昌久（ごいまさひさ）

　１９１６年（大正５年）１１月
２２日、東京に生まれる。詩人、
哲学者、著述家、音楽家。
　青年のころ、音楽家への道を志
すが、自然に哲学や精神世界を求
めるようになる。１９４９年（昭
和２４年）３０歳で神我一体を経
験し、覚者となる。
　平和についての著書・詩集は５０冊以上あり、英語は
もとより他言語へも翻訳されている。主な著書は、「神
と人間」、「天と地をつなぐもの」、「老子講義」、「聖書講
義」、「霊性の開発」など。

　１９５５年、すべての宗教、社会、民族、政治などの
壁を越えて、祈りによる世界平和運動を全世界的に展開
する。国内、国外に共鳴者多数。
　１９８０年（昭和５５年）８月１７日逝去さる。

　世界人類が平和でありますように

About the Author

Masahisa Goi

Born in Tokyo, Japan on November 22, 1916, Masahisa Goi was a poet, philosopher, writer and singer.

In his early years he aimed at a career in music, but found himself spontaneously drawn to the areas of philosophy and human guidance. At the age of thirty he attained oneness with his divine self.

Mr. Goi authored more than fifty books and volumes of poetry, including God and Man (his first and most classic work), One Who Joins the Earth with the Sky, The Spirit of Lao Tsu, Essays on the Bible, How to Develop your Spirituality, and others.

In 1955 he founded a worldwide movement of prayer for world peace transcending religious, social, and political barriers.

He departed from this world on August 17, 1980.

May Peace Prevail on Earth.